A few years ago, when I wrote *A Schizoaffective's Brief Guide to Thriving with Schizophrenia*, I was not expecting it to be nearly as well received as it has been. I have loved getting feedback stating how much reading about my experiences has helped others. Since then, I have been playing with the idea of releasing a longer edition, but always shied away because I feel that the one-hour read format gives the book a level of accessibility that I do not want to diminish.

However, I feel that there is one aspect of the original book that was glossed over far too quickly. The delusions and the constant anxiety they produce are, in my experience, by far the most awful and debilitating aspect of this disorder, and also the hardest for friends and loved ones to understand.

So in that light, I'd like to take another crack at explaining the sort of phenomenological manifestation that I have experienced in my own recovery from schizophrenia. If you're just picking up this book, and have not read A Schizoaffective's Brief Guide to

Thriving with Schizophrenia, I recommend you read it first. It is a much more broad overview of the Schizoaffective and Schizophrenia disorders as a whole, and this book is intended as a supplement to it. The first book was more about coping techniques and tactics. In this second book, I focus more on the phenomenon of delusions and paranoia to help those suffering from it gain insight and seek help, and aid loved ones to understand and assist.

Before I begin, I'd like to reiterate that everything I say should be taken with a grain of salt. I am not a medical professional, but I was diagnosed with schizoaffective disorder a decade ago. Since then, I've managed to recover most of my life, graduate college in engineering, and live a fairly normal life. This is an explanation of how I've sort of rationalized my way through an experience most would consider horrifying and generally irrational.

Keep in mind that this is also only my experience. The sample size of this survey is one. Everyone will be different, but I suspect everyone is also the same in a lot of ways. It's up to the reader to sort out what those similarities are.

My goal in this book, perhaps even more so than the last, is to help provide people with similar experiences to me with the initial insights needed for them to manage their lives with this phenomenon. This experience is horrifying, both for the person living it, and those around them who care. It is navigable and with the right help, it can be managed. But to do that, one needs to rationalize their way through what they're experiencing and have experienced. This requires a certain amount of self-awareness that I hope to impart upon my readers, as they find similarities and differences between their own experience and mine.

Something I stressed in the original book, that I cannot stress enough, is as a schizophrenic or a loved one of one, you need to change your understanding of schizophrenia to match what you are experiencing. Everyone has a mental picture of the disorder, and it's usually horribly wrong, thanks in part to hack writers and authors misrepresenting it in fiction, and the occasional pundit or politician weaponizing the idea of us during partisan jockeying. Don't believe what you've seen on TV or read in a "True" crime novel. Redefine your understanding of the meaning of the disorder to align with the things you are experiencing that negatively impact your life. A huge takeaway I hope to impart in these two books is just an ability for fellow schizophrenics to recognize their own symptoms, because once we can recognize our symptoms, and start to understand our symptoms, coping becomes easier, and when coping becomes easier, recovery becomes possible.

What are delusions

My understanding of the medical definition of delusion is that it is any deeply held belief that is not commonly shared elsewhere in society. I think this is a rather diminishing and politically minded definition, and one that I take great philosophical objection to, especially when I am lost in delusions. It allows for the more bizarre beliefs that are baked into many religions and popular conspiracy theories to get a pass, and then targets the individual's personal beliefs an individual forms themself, regardless of the truth. By this definition, Galileo was delusional. By this definition, delusion is synonymous with blasphemy.

But don't get me wrong, delusions can be horrible, hellish things to live with. Left unchecked, they make things as simple as going to the grocery store feel like close encounters with death, or worse.

Delusions, as I treat them in my own life, are ideas, either newly formed or deeply held, that induce a state of intense paranoia within me. I chose this as my definition, because it makes them more easily recognized, and because I believe that the paranoia inducing ones are the ones that cause problems for my well-being.

The medical definition functions better as a diagnostic tool for medical professionals. My definition is a much more practical understanding for someone suffering from delusions looking for insight and improvements that help lead to recovery.

What is paranoia

Paranoia, in my experience, is intense distrust and anxiety, and it is the core of delusions, as I define them. Paranoia is feeling that you're being misled, manipulated, spied on, or used, often as a means to a horrifying end. It is the feeling a delusion produces, and it can be both rational and irrational. To those of us experiencing them, they always feel rational, although we may often know that other people will not see them that way, so we often suffer in silence with these deep paranoias and delusions and few people around us even know. When we do open up, it's like trying to explain a sprawling new universe, and the nuances of everything are lost. Those are the ones people are most familiar with.

The paranoias I experience the most now are much smaller in scope, I believe because I catch them earlier. They can be triggered by the most mundane of things. Sometimes when an ambulance drives by me headed the other way, I get horrified that I caused some sort of accident behind me. It's irrational, I know I didn't. I'd remember if I did. But these paranoias like to grab onto the smallest unknowns and fill them with the worst-case scenario.

One of the most important things to realize is, not everything is related. Most things have nothing to do with you personally. I think something that gets conditioned into us by fiction is that everything has meaning and is related to the plot experienced by the point of view character. But in the real world, it isn't.

It's hard to avoid this kind of thinking, especially when we are dealing with hearing voices, either from hallucination, or the sort of gap-filling voices that come from eavesdropping or half hearing conversations. But we have to actively work and break down the logic of what we're hearing and be mindful of our thoughts. We need to purposefully take inventory of the facts and recognize what information we're missing.

These missing pieces are rarely the worst-case scenarios we imagine. If we let these worst-case scenarios haunt us, we imprison ourselves in a nightmare. I know from living in the nightmare myself that I always felt like I had to stay. I had to fight, because if I abandoned it, horrible things would keep happening. And a lot of my paranoia and delusions were about things that really do happen, they just were not actually happening to me or the people I was concerned about.

The stages of psychosis

I have read that psychosis comes in three phases. Starting with a prodrome, a period of withdrawal from social activities and school, where the individual struggles with distractions, depression, irritability, and inability to differentiate between their own thoughts and what others are saying.

The second phase is called the acute phase is when the more widely known delusions, disorganized speech and hallucinations set in.

And the third phase is the recovery phase when the other symptoms fade, with the help of medication and therapy.

I don't disagree with this assessment, but I do think the line between the prodrome and the acute phase is far more blurred than it appears in what I have read.

For me, the social and professional withdrawal was a product of delusion and paranoia that had already set in, but was not being vocalized, at least not in depth or frequently. The frequent distraction was the effect of hyper vigilance, from feelings of extreme distrust of everyone around me. The same can be said for lack of sleep, depression, and irritability. The difficulty in differentiating my own thoughts was because I was hearing voices that sounded like the people in the room were talking. Catatonic behaviors are also a product of it. When trying to ignore the hallucinations, one often ends up ignoring real things as well. The acute phase to me is less a distinct thing from the prodrome, as it is the point where all the compounding effects of the delusion-paranoia feedback loop, which I'll discuss later, reach an extreme where they cannot be hidden anymore by myself, or ignored anymore by the people around me.

How (I think) delusions form

My delusions started as a defense mechanism that kept me from suicide. It's an odd thing to recognize, considering how long they haunted me and how they almost brought me to suicide.

I became delusional after a horrible breakup. The woman I dated in college, as it turned out, was already dating someone when I met her. He was in boot camp the first six months of my relationship with her, so he could only communicate with her using letters. She never told me about him until we got back from a school break and he started calling her every day before his shift. She told me he was just her best friend. And I did my best to believe her, while waking up every morning to his accursed phone calls. They had me in a bind. It wasn't cheating because he was God knows how far away, so they weren't doing anything physical. He was just her best friend. But it quickly became so obvious that he wasn't. Then she had to choose between us. And all I heard about was everything I was doing wrong in the relationship. I didn't tell her she was beautiful enough. I split checks with her because I was a broke. I didn't buy her gifts, and when I did, it was only because she was asking me to or it was a holiday. Then one day she told me she chose me and started asking me if I planned to marry her after college. I told her we'll cross that bridge when we get to it. A week later, she dumped me and flew across the country to be with him. When she came back, she went back to me. We did that for months, until I had the strength to break it off with her.

I blamed myself. If only I had more perfectly done the things she asked… bought more gifts, made her feel more special…etc. The entire last few months of the relationship, I had spent my time trying to get high and drunk enough to not care what was happening, so I could focus enough to do my schoolwork. I was in my junior year of engineering college, which many people consider to be the most difficult of the five. (Note to parents, no one gets a STEM degree from a state school in four years anymore, unless they have priority registration thanks to a disability or athletic program. No one can get all the classes they need when they need them. They're full before you're even allowed to register.)

By the time we broke up, I was already living in an elaborate fantasy. I couldn't bring myself to accept that she had manipulated and lied to me for so long that my mind fashioned an elaborate alternate reality that allowed her to remain who I wanted her to be. The world of unknowns and horrifying worst-case scenarios was born.

The delusion-paranoia feedback loop

I created an elaborate narrative to explain how my ex really did still love me. This quickly took on a far greater scope than the two of us and expanded to encompass a hellish conspiracy spanning the whole of civilization, within which we were a small negligible piece.

How did it get that far? Paranoia and delusion form a feedback loop. Delusions make us afraid, hypervigilant, constantly scheming and rationalizing on the worst-case scenario. With every new piece of information we receive, a tree of horrible possibilities grows. All of this sends us deeper and deeper into a state of hypervigilance and anxiety.

This anxiety then breeds schizophrenia's other symptoms. The taunting, oppressive voices, hallucinations, false recognitions of people both in person and in photographs. Sleep deprivation from anxiety feeds into all of it even more. Self-medication with drugs exacerbates and fuels the mix. When the paranoia builds to a certain point, an avalanche of delusion and self-destruction is unleashed.

Something that I believe is tragically left out of discussion in the treatment plans of many people with schizophrenia is treatment for PTSD. Society at large still seems to think that PTSD is only for veterans and sexual abuse victims, failing to recognize that the delusion of mortal danger produces the same level of stress as actual mortal danger, and I feel should be treated similarly. Another aspect that I think applies in my case, and likely other schizophrenics and schizoaffectives, is a phenomenon with growing recognition known as PISD. PISD is a not yet recognized disorder built on the observation that infidelity can trigger PTSD-like symptoms with varying severity based on just how traumatic the relationship was. It is not a recognized disorder, currently, but I, and many others, feel that they've lived it. It's fairly accepted now that emotionally abusive relationships can trigger PTSD. A newer diagnosis of CPTSD (Complex Post Traumatic Stress Disorder) for emotional abuse is becoming known in some therapies. Something that I'd hope the public becomes more aware of, is that infidelity may just be the tip of an emotional-abuse iceberg, and survivors of emotional abuse are often every bit as blind to it as the people around them, until it causes a complete mental breakdown. There is a risk that the diagnosis may be overlooked, and the survivor receives a sort of catchall diagnosis, like bipolar or schizophrenia or the like.

Self-diagnosis is always dangerous and generally frowned upon, but at least in the American healthcare system, getting in front of a psychiatrist takes weeks or months, and one is often only there for an hour before a diagnosis is stamped on. All the expertise in the world isn't going to succeed without information and context. If you asked Albert Einstein to solve a basic seventh grade algebra problem, but never showed it to him, he couldn't do it. He'd just be making a wild guess. That's the biggest flaw with American healthcare, in my opinion. Psychiatrists are being tasked with diagnosing individuals who don't trust them, and therefore aren't being honest, and, on top of that, don't actually know or understand what's going on with themselves.

To get the diagnosis right, we have to step back, look at what we're experiencing and have experienced, and work with the psychiatrist. We're there to use their expertise. They're our employee. Their job is to help us, and to do that, they need to understand us. Unfortunately, we're working against a clock that provides limited time. It's paramount to be honest with ourselves and the psychiatrist.

That all being said, I do still believe I have schizoaffective disorder, because I have always and continue to hear voices on some level and am prone to crafting elaborate narratives. I believe I have both a stress disorder and this underlying disorder that blended together to form the hellish nightmare I lived in ten years ago, and that I am still coping with.

Interaction with other Schizophrenia Symptoms

The delusion and paranoia feedback loop is greatly affected by the other symptoms I experience. Left unchecked, they all feed together to strengthen and further the delusional narrative.

In A *Schizoaffective's Brief Guide to Thriving with Schizophrenia,* I laid out and defined how I experienced Thought Voices, Gap Filling Voices, False Recognitions and Visual Hallucinations, but due to the desire for brevity did not fully elaborate on how interconnected they all are with each other and the delusion-paranoia feedback loop.

I'll start by breaking down thought voices. The way I have come to understand the most common kind of voice I hear, is that it is my own imagination of what other people are thinking or would say about whatever I am presently thinking at the moment. When I am feeling horribly down or depressed, or anxious about myself, these voices taunt and harass me. But that's not always what they do.

When I am trapped in the delusion-paranoia loop, my mind is locked into a massive, long running thought experiment, about some hypothetical horror. I find myself trying to figure out not just my place in it, but also the place of my friends, my family, late night talk-show hosts, the President, just about everyone. This imagined narrative plays out in my head in the form of these people talking to each other. It is vivid and fluid and so powerful that it seems almost like they are actually saying these things, or thinking these things, having these conversations elsewhere, behind my back.

And if I allow myself to believe that what I am imagining is not an imaginary hypothetical, but some magical form of clairvoyance, it launches me deep into the delusion-paranoia loop. Because not only does it mean I'm taking flawed hypothetical concepts as fact, but it also means that as events continue to play out, I start thinking everyone around me is lying to me, manipulating and gaslighting me. Because I'm hearing all these conversations that are being had behind my back. I think I know what they are doing and am completely wrong. This causes their actions to not line up with what I thought about them, and as I start trying to reconcile these facts, the facts of how these people are actually acting, vs how I believe they are acting in my symptomatic moments of false clairvoyance, I find myself considering even more horrible possibilities, and creating very paranoid mental versions of the people I should be relying on most.

It produces the most horrible feeling of isolation and betrayal, because I do not believe I can trust anyone.

I personally do not experience the full-blown visual out-of-body experiences other schizophrenics I have met have described, but I imagine those experiences often play out similarly to the audio dramas I experience.

Gap filling voices also take on a very insidious role during the delusion-paranoia feedback loop. Gap filling voices are when I am actually hearing a real person talking, but because it's coming through a wall, or on a half private phone call, or some other eavesdropping situation, I am not able to hear all of it and my mind starts filling in the gaps and it usually fills them in with terrifying notions that play into the delusional narrative. This one can be particularly insidious, because if I am overhearing, say, a phone conversation between a concerned roommate and some unknown party, where they are talking about me, the horrifying gap-filling can become particularly powerful.

The third type of hallucination I experience is much more subtle, but equally able to spark delusion is false recognition. I see a face that is similar to someone and then I think it is that person. This may seem harmless, but it can feed into delusions and paranoias in very insidious ways. Strangers on the street look like acquaintances, and if they have a generic face, appear frequently enough to feel like I'm being stalked. Friends become movie stars. Ex-lovers become porn stars. Every false recognition, if allowed to be ruminated on, can manufacture a false explanation, which feeds the false narrative of delusion.

Another thing to keep in mind is that a lot of people lump schizophrenia in with psychopathy or sociopathy. because they have no idea what schizophrenia is, and their understanding has been warped heavily by hack writers and filmmakers who have no idea what schizophrenia is, and lack the imagination to come up with a convincing backstory for their villain.

People with schizophrenia do not lack empathy (like psycho and sociopaths) but it may appear that way because the delusions and voices warp the phenomenon of empathy. Empathy isn't some telepathic ability that lets people understand what others are feeling without context. It's a rational thought process. It's informed subconsciously by reading body language, yes, but there is a very large thought experiment aspect in which one examines what they know about what another person knows, and values, and makes a best guess at what that other person is feeling and thinking.

When I'm lost in a delusional parallel reality, the assumptions about the other person's knowledge are out of alignment. If I seem to lack empathy, it's because my anticipation is founded on flawed premises. Recovery only really comes in earnest when the premises are worked out. Unfortunately for our loved ones, that process needs to be worked out slowly and on its own.

The Logic of Delusions

People who've never experienced delusions tend to believe that delusions are random and irrational. And in doing so, they fail to see the experience of delusions. In philosophical logic, what's known as an argument can be broken apart into three steps. There's the premise, something like, shape A is a square. Then there's the inference, squares are a special type of rectangle. Then there's the conclusion, in this case, shape A is a square and a rectangle.

The way I've come to understand delusions is, they are in many ways, massive sprawling arguments, which barrel forward towards conclusions that are incomprehensible to anyone other than the delusional person(s) experiencing it, and the other symptoms of schizophrenia are triggered by the stress it causes to create an avalanche effect of paranoid reinforcement.

Here's an example of the effect in action. Keep in mind while reading this that I am writing a hypothetical here, so you can see the effect in action. There are a couple of jumps in the logic but jumps like that occur when under the extreme stress that creates delusions, especially when hallucinations are in play.

Premise, my girlfriend is cheating on me. If she is cheating on me, then she has been lying to me. If she has been lying to me so well for so long, then I cannot tell when she is lying to me. If I cannot tell when she is lying to me, then I cannot tell when other people are lying to me as well. If I cannot tell when people are lying, then everything I've ever been told could be a lie. Conclusion, I must logically examine everything everyone has told or will tell me and check for ulterior motives that may lead to lies.

Then schizophrenia steps in with a delusional premise. This adult film performer looks a lot like my ex-girlfriend. If this is her, then either she is doing this consensually, or she isn't. Some of the films she has made depict things I do not believe she would consent to. If she is not consenting to this, then she needs help. If she needs help, then this danger may be life threatening. I should ask the police for help.

Next premise. The police sent me for psychiatric evaluation when I tried to get their help. They didn't do anything. If they didn't do anything, they must be complicit in the crime. If they're complicit, they are crooked. If the police are crooked, then criminal networks control more of society than we are led to believe.

And from here, you may see some of the extremes that this line of reasoning inevitably reaches. When all of society could be corrupt, and no one is ever actually capable of knowing if they're being lied to, extremes as absurd as the notion that earth is a farm used by aliens to raise human livestock are within the realm of what can eventually be reached. All from a simple premise built on mistaken identity. Bear in mind that, throughout this snowball, the auditory hallucination mind-reading effect steps in to reinforce everything. The more a person racks their brain trying to figure out what everyone else is thinking, the more parallel versions of these people start to form. When the expectation of their behavior does not conform with what is observed, an explanation is created. They're terrified. They're lying to me. Why are they lying to me? They're complicit. Why are they complicit? Either they are being bribed or extorted or both.

It creates a feeling of complete isolation and loneliness. The experience of compassion and empathy stops coming from real people. They've had enough. The only listening and caring help comes from inside your own head, from the voices, from the fictional creations built off of former friends, family, acquaintances and lovers.

And within all of that, there's a sort of sunk-cost fallacy keeping a delusional person going. They've lost so much pursuing the delusion that abandoning the delusions feels not only like abandoning the victims of their cause but also like there is no going back. Too many bridges were burned. And it's extremely rough. Because embracing that you're wrong means embracing that all these people you think secretly are helping from the shadows actually aren't.

But the thing you've got to realize is they are trying to help. They do care. But not about the fiction you've created. They care about you. They just have no idea what to do, because they've never experienced what you're experiencing.

The delusional conclusions may be completely logical. The inferences may be sound, but the premises are the problem. The bedrock of an entire delusional hell world may be just one single inaccurate fact. And it will take a lot of time to sort out exactly which premises were real, and which weren't. Also, you may have noticed some sort of oversized logic jumps or plot holes in the hypothetical I gave. Again, delusions typically form as sprawling though experiments. Sometimes writing them down, as crazy as they may look, helps one to spot the places where jumps and false premises may have snuck in. This is another reason why I have found turning my delusions into fictional stories has helped me process them.

Something to keep in mind while working one's way out of delusions is the simple math of probabilities. A sprawling delusion is a web of "if this, then probably this." Even if every link of the web is considered a high probability, like 80%, the odds of the conclusions are still low. If 20 linkages are needed to support the conclusion, and each link is only 80% likely to be true, then there is a 0.8 to the 20th power chance of the delusion being true. That only comes out to 1.1%. There would be a 98.9% chance that somewhere along the way, a link was not true, causing the nightmare-narrative web to break down.

We might then be wondering, if we cannot understand the world through a network of logical conclusions and assumptions, how are we to know anything? How does anyone have a worldview? How do "sane" people all construct and agree on roughly the same reality?

The answer to that is trust. We trust our friends and family. We have faith in our close personal relationships. Because our people also have trust and faith in other people we personally may have never met, society forms this sort of web where interpersonal faith constructs a shared understanding of everything.

Is the common understanding right about everything? Probably not. Is it perfectly just for everyone? No. But it has something that an individual does not have. Millions of eyes. Millions of ears, millions of minds discussing and sharing and cooperating. Because of this, the probabilities of each of its links are greater than the ones an individual perceives.

However, something else that has to be kept in mind is that the "shared understanding," as I called it, is not a uniform agreement. It has currents, and subcultures, and places where cultures themselves may start to break off, and form areas of shared delusion.

Cultural interplay

Delusions are not randomly formed in a vacuum. In my experience, they have formed around interests and life experiences. They are parallel narrative arcs that weave through both real and hallucinated events, often built heavily on assumptions related to the behaviors of other people when they are outside my ability to observe. They feed on the unknowns of life, and often other people can fuel them instead of dull them.

At this point, I'm sure everyone is aware of the massive span of online conspiracy theories, and may have a slight inkling into the myriads of networks of people subscribing to, postulating on, and outright believing the endless seas of what I have come to accept are cultural delusions.

While I certainly don't believe the government and our news broadcasts are telling the complete truth all the time; I have found that real conspiracy is much more bureaucratic, dry, and banal than the sprawling absurdity that is peddled online, and those friends who like to peddle in such theories are usually getting their information if not directly from the internet, secondhand or third hand from the internet.

I'm not going to dive into refuting any of the ones I've heard, for both the practicality of not diving into a 20,000 word tangent and the fact that whatever ones I bothered to refute would probably be outdated, abandoned, and have evolved into something new in a couple of years.

Surprisingly, something I think that really helped me pull my mind out of these conspiratorial tracks were two (very long winded and dense) non-fiction books I read while doing research for sprawling conspiratorial novels I was writing. *Active Measures* by Thomas Rid, and *You've Been Played* by Adrian Hon. The key takeaways I got from them were that often the leaks of information we get online, that serve as the launching point for conspiracies, are subtly fraudulent. The source of the information is not who they say they were, and often these huge data dumps include forgeries deliberately crafted to spark conspiracy theories. These theories often spread in a sort of gamified way, through networks akin to multilevel marketing pyramid schemes crossed with role-playing games. What makes a conspiracy theory spread is less the underlying truth of such a theory and more the social currency it provides. They're interesting and fun to talk about, and have a certain amount of shock value. I look at conspiracy theories less like things that may be happening and more like a form of entertainment that blurs reality with a compelling fictional narrative arc.

If I seem to be downplaying the danger here, it is because I want people to understand that this is what makes a theory spread, replicate and evolve. But what makes them so damaging and dangerous is that they join into the delusion-paranoia feedback loop and provide it with reinforcement. Many people who believe conspiracy theories believe they are some separate thing they know about, but are keeping themselves out of. To "normal" people, they're fun, in the way horror movies are fun, but the schizophrenic paranoia-delusion feedback loop leads one to weave their own life through the context of the conspiracy theory. So while everyone else is eating popcorn and enjoying the horror movie from across the fourth wall, the person with schizophrenia finds oneself a character within it.

When I was lost in delusion, I did not see conspiracies as some irrelevant background, but rather a driving current that had directly caused so many things in my life. The communities that form around and peddle these theories are fuel for the fire, because not only do they tell you things are happening, they believe the things you tell them are happening.

It forms a cycle that one cannot simply snap out of, and unfortunately medication alone rarely will completely break a person free from delusional thinking. My experience with the medication has been that it does little to change my thoughts, and more just makes me apathetic about them enough that they no longer stress me out, which helps break the anxiety driven paranoia cycle of symptoms feeding off each other, but did not resolve the delusions creating the anxiety themselves.

For me, the only thing that broke me out of was forming an awareness of myself, and the context of the world around me, but with it is also an understanding that there is no objective truth. In school, they like to talk about enlightenment and the allegory of the cave, but I don't believe any such state can exist. Believing you know or understand everything is just another delusion.

To me, enlightenment means knowing we may be wrong and being willing to adjust our understanding on any new evidence.

But we also must always look at evidence and understand what it is, who is saying it and where it came from before we accept it as a premise and use it to extrapolate any conclusions from it.

Breaking the cycle

What broke me out of the cycle of self-destruction was outside intervention. Parents and friends who cared about me enough to get me into inpatient treatment. As demeaning as the experience is, months in a relatively low stress environment, with regular therapy, both individual and group, medication, sobriety, and my own ambition, broke me out of my first avalanche. But it wasn't the only one. By my count, I've had four in the last ten years, each significantly less intense than the last. The first one was the only which required in-patient care, but I continue to see a therapist bi-weekly and a psychiatrist periodically.

That being said, all the outside intervention on earth would have been wasted if I hadn't opened myself to the possibility that I was misinterpreting things. Being involuntarily hospitalized and medicated is a terrifying experience in itself. Especially when I already believed that there was some massive fascist conspiracy attempting to silence me. Disheartening as it may be for many people to hear, it took years for me to break out of the cycle. I don't think I was really starting to come out of it until seven years in, when I finally accepted my diagnosis instead of fighting it. That was when the inspiration occurred that led me to write A Schizoaffective's Brief Guide to Thriving with Schizophrenia. This was despite having been out of the hospital for years, finishing college, finding employment and seeming to live normally.

What made me able to function all those years, and what led me to greater insight into what was going on with me, was less a breakthrough out of the delusions and more of a strategic decision on my part within the delusion.

I knew that I could not help with the issues I was imagining from jail or a hospital. I knew no one was going to listen to me or help me if they thought I was "crazy." So I decided to live my life by the uncertainty principle. I looked at everything from the perspective that I was both wrong and not wrong simultaneously. Which seemed a very overwhelming thing to do, but it was more like I was in a waiting posture. Waiting for some external event to confirm my hypothesis, because all my experiments had failed, and were destroying my life. I'm not saying it was easy. I was terrified most of the time. Panic attacks used to be a daily thing for me. Almost no one knew that because I seemed tired and bored most of the time. This was actually because I was either exhausted from panicking or when I was panicking, I was spaced out and catatonic, wearing a very good poker face.

But beyond that, the basic principles of mental wellness still apply to people with schizophrenia and schizoaffective disorder and are every bit as vital as medication and therapy. For me, the first time, the paranoia and delusions started because I had lost all joy in life. I felt like I had no reason to live, and a delusion formed to fill that gap.

This means finding hobbies that are affordable enough to be available at all times. For me the go to is writing. Aside from these short guides, I write science fiction, using it to sort of twist my delusions into narrative fiction. This conversion helps me keep them filed in the not-true category and also acts as a sort of always-available therapist in a way. I also garden during the growing season and cook my own meals whenever I can. But these are the things that work for me, because they are the things I enjoy. For some people it's reading books, for others it's drawing, doing yoga or running marathons. Only you know what you like to do. Find as many things as you can and start looking at the things that are not particularly expensive. Also, keep in mind that consumerism doesn't actually increase enjoyment. You don't need a $2000 pencil set to enjoy drawing if you actually love drawing. You don't need $500 yoga pants to enjoy yoga if you actually enjoy yoga. If you can afford those things, by all means splurge, but if you can't, don't let not having them hold you back.

Another thing to keep in mind, stress is your worst enemy. Anxiety breeds paranoia. A transformational realization I had was when I figured out that I have panic attacks. I'd always thought they were these huge dramatic things where people hyperventilate or cry or frantically run around. I don't do those things. When I have a panic attack, I go catatonic. Everyone around me thinks I've just spaced out and stopped paying attention. Actually, I'm sitting there with a poker face on while my mind is racing about a million horrible what ifs, wanting to go run away and cry, but knowing that would only make things worse. When I realized that these bouts of stress-induced shutdown were panic attacks, I was able to start identifying the things that caused the panic and head them off.

Other helpful advice

You're not alone in this. Millions of people have schizophrenia, schizoaffective disorder, and many other disorders that also cause delusions and hallucinations. There likely are support groups in your community for helping people recover from this sort of thing. From medical group therapy to addiction recovery groups like AA, NA, and SMART Recovery.

There are also organizations for family members or friends who want to get involved and learn how to better support someone in crisis through to recovery. My parents took NAMI Family to Family classes.

Stress is the enemy, and addiction is stress. If you're addicted to a substance, not having it will make you feel anxious and uneasy. Something I believed, both when I was smoking marijuana, and after when I was smoking cigarettes, was that smoking always made me feel relaxed. Sobriety was stressful. That's the subtle hook of addiction. You think the drug is relieving your anxiety, but actually the absence of it is the source of your stress. Every time you come down, you're uneasy until you're able to go up again. That unease breeds the other symptoms.

Marijuana's other effects also work to intensify delusion and paranoia. The phenomenon of people "sketching out" on weed is well known among stoners. It can lock you into paranoia loops that last until you come down, but if you're already in a delusional cycle, the paranoia just builds on what you're already experiencing. It also makes you more likely to make the sort of logical jumps that further delusions.

Illegal drugs of any kind also bring with them extreme external stress. During my time of heavy marijuana use, there was a cop who hung out two houses over from our house. His presence had nothing to do with us. He was parked near a stop sign on a busy road, and was trying to give people tickets for running it. Judging from his siren whoops, he'd catch two or three people every day he chilled there, and was there pretty much every other day. But he stressed the crap out of me, because he would park between me and my dealer's house, which meant it wasn't uncommon for me to walk by with a large quantity of weed in my backpack.

Those short walks past his squad car were terrifying, even though I knew he was just looking for cars running the stop sign. Because there's this nagging thought about what if he isn't? That's the kind of nagging paranoia delusions grab onto. The paranoid aspect of schizophrenia comes up with other reasons for him to be there. In my case, I thought he was spying on me. Then I'm thinking my house is bugged. Then I'm wondering why they haven't busted us yet. Then I start wondering if he's secretly there to protect me. Not in the normal cop protect sense but in some huge larger conspiratorial sense. The farther down the paranoid train of thought one goes, the more delusions get tacked on and paranoias form, and it starts from basic mortal fears. Illegal drug use creates existential fear of police, and my mind rationalizes that fear in very creative ways.

If you want to escape paranoia and fear, you need to drop all the avoidable stresses that you can. In pursuing this, I've also dropped coffee and energy drinks. Not long after I first realized I was having frequent panic attacks, my office ran out of regular coffee. So, I drank decaf for two months, because regular took that long to get restocked. A couple weeks in, I noticed the number of panic attacks I was having dropped dramatically. When the normal stuff came back in, I drank it, and the panic attacks came back. So, I've quit regular coffee. It's not much of a sacrifice. After a couple weeks of adjustment, I've found my energy levels are the same as when I was drinking caffeine. Addiction and tolerance can happen with anything, even culturally accepted drugs.

A useful thing to keep in mind with substances is the phenomenons of tolerance and dependence. I consider addiction to be when I'm dependent on something to not feel anxious, and not feel stressed, and when I'm so tolerant to that substance that being on some level of it feels normal.

When high is normal, you're getting no benefit from being high anymore, but it's causing your sober time to be unpleasant. Also, being high all the time is absurdly expensive, both in lost job opportunities and actual cost of the drugs, on your wallet and your physical and mental health.

Beating addiction is rough, but it can be done. If you need help, I recommend looking for resources in your community and asking loved ones for help.

The other thing I can never stress enough is the danger of lapsing during addiction recovery. Tolerance builds quickly, but it also drops off even faster. Several people I've met during recovery died of overdose because they tried to go hard during a lapse. Don't be another one. Recovery is a marathon, not a sprint, and lapsing is an (undesirable) part of recovery, but it is by far the most dangerous part.

Causes of schizophrenia

This is a subject I thought was best to shy away from, for a few reasons. Mainly because the science is not out on it. Studies exist linking it to everything from genetics, to bacterial infections from cat bites and poop, to prenatal diets, to drug use, and to pesticide or other chemical exposure. There are literally too many theories to count and at this point in time it's all speculation.

My personal speculation is that it's caused by a perfect storm of converging factors, and simultaneously is a bit of a catchall disorder that throws a wide net and encompasses a broad spectrum of problems that manifest themselves in similar ways.

For that reason, it's important to remember that what I say works for me or feels a certain way for me is not necessarily correct for you. This disease isn't like having a broken leg. It varies, and even if it didn't, there isn't a one-size fits all cast for every kind of broken leg either.

I'm only bringing this up because my mother has on several occasions expressed guilt, and that she blames herself for my illness, because of things she's read about one very specific theory on what causes this disorder. And she shouldn't. There was a perfect storm of conditions that made me this way, and I don't really think anything she or anyone could've done would've stopped it.

So, family members, please don't blame yourselves. To use diabetes as a metaphor, nobody ever caught diabetes because they got cake on their birthdays. Some were born with it. Some had a lifetime of sodas and donuts and ice cream candy coming in along with the cake. There's a lot more going on than this one theory you're researching. There may be truth to it, but I don't think this disorder has a smoking gun. It has an ecosystem. Skateboarding is linked to broken bones. Does skateboarding always cause a broken bone? No. Are all broken bones caused by skateboarding? No. Keep that in mind if curiosity leads you to dig online trying to find a cause for your case of schizophrenia. Generally, people don't think chronic depression or bipolar disorder has a singular cause. We should consider schizophrenia the same way.

And if I may take the opportunity to get on a soapbox a little bit, there is another note I think I should make. I feel any claims of genetic links should be taken with a grain of salt. While genetics may hold a role in any disorder, the type of statistical analysis that uncovers these correlations easily falls prey to correlation versus causation fallacies. For example, imagine a culture somewhere whose traditional foods heavily use a little studied spice unique to their culture. That spice causes a specific kind of cancer if consumed heavily for many years. A genetic study related to that specific cancer would find that genes specific to members of that culture were predisposed to that specific cancer.

This type of error is harmful if scientists do not do their due diligence, and if the wider world does not behave ethically. Which unfortunately is a tall order.

Studies have shown schizophrenia in America is more common among Latino and African American populations. A genetic study of schizophrenia may then link specific genes unique to those races to the disorder, when in actuality the cause may be environmental.

When I developed schizophrenia, I was living in a college slum. All of my residences had black mold infestations, including the dorms. The landlords would charge us for mold cleanups that were never performed. I know because I worked for a painting company, and at one point found myself in my old apartment painting over the very mold I had been charged to repair a year earlier. Considering all the other apartments I painted, this was standard practice citywide. I have since developed schizophrenia, and around the same time that my symptoms developed, one of my former roommates developed brain cancer and has since passed. Is it linked? No one can really say. Black mold exposure wasn't his or my only risk factor. But there are numerous environmental hazards that are more prominent in minority communities. Couple that with the realities of surviving in poverty and gang violence, and it may very well be true that impoverished communities have a much higher rate of stress disorders, which may sometimes be mistaken for, or contribute to, the development of schizophrenia.

I'm not saying there is harm in seeking correlations. Maybe it's just the paranoia in me from studying the history of how people with mental health diagnosis like mine used to be treated, but I fear that these false genetic correlations may lead to proactive measures of a dystopian nature.

Send-off

Delusions and paranoia are horrifying. It is their nature, it's what they are. I hope that by reading this book, I have helped you begin to understand them, as I have begun to understand, because that understanding has helped me escape them.

It won't be easy, but take some comfort in knowing that the worst is probably already behind you. If something led you to pick up this book, then you're probably already aware on some level that delusions and paranoia are affecting your life, and they never affect it for the better. That awareness is the first step out of the hell the delusions convince you you're in. Keep going. It's never too late to repair your life.

Thank you for reading, and please, leave a review!

https://www.amazon.com/review/create-review/?ie=UTF8&channel=glance-detail&asin=B0D8Z5FTSF

And if you haven't already, check out *A Schizoaffective's Brief Guide to Thriving with Schizophrenia*

https://www.amazon.com/dp/B08XC2NF5R

A Schizoaffective's Brief Guide to Navigating Delusions and Paranoia

By Anonymous
Copyright © 2024
Self-published

The cover was designed using resources from Freepik.com

Made in the USA
Columbia, SC
04 December 2024

48413830R00028